DEFENDER
OF THE FAITH

10 WEIRD FACTS ABOUT THE CORONATION

RAY COMFORT

Newber

Defender of the Faith

Bridge-Logos, Inc.
Newberry, FL 32669, USA

Edited by Lynn Copeland

Page design and production by Genesis Group

ISBN 978-1-61036-300-6

Library of Congress Control Number: 2022948045

Printed in India

CONTENTS

*"The king's heart is in the
hand of the LORD,
like the rivers of water;
He turns it wherever He wishes."*

(Proverbs 21:1)

CHAPTER ONE

DEFENDER
OF FAITH?

In a world of depressingly bad news, the crowning of a king is a breath of fresh air in an oxygen-starved room. A coronation isn't anything like a presidential inauguration, an eclipse of the moon, or a night at the Oscars. It is a finger-licking smorgasbord of glorious sights and sounds, ecstatic crowds, a golden coach, a crown that is pregnant with the world's most precious diamonds, an ancient throne, a golden pearl-encrusted scepter, an array of gorgeous apparel, presidents, celebrities, splendid color, and soul-stirring trumpets fit for the ears of a king. It is truly a spectacular once-in-lifetime experience.

One big question that was on the minds of those in the royal know was, "What will Charles do with the title 'Defender of the Faith'?" The world has radically changed since the 1953 coronation of Queen Elizabeth, and such a title doesn't fit as comfortably on his shoulders as it did on his dear mother's.

Defender of *the* Faith. What does that even mean? Shouldn't *all* faiths be defended? And why is the sovereign of England given such a strange title?

Five hundred years ago, in October 1521, Pope Leo X conferred on King Henry VIII the title "Defender of the Faith." The king was being rewarded for his promotion of the Catholic Church. This was very timely, because it happened during the developing Protestant Reformation, led by a rogue monk named Martin Luther.

The Pope gave Henry the title after he published a book called *The Defense of the Seven Sacraments*. In it the king defended the seven major doctrines of the Catholic Church against the criticisms of the rebellious monk. Henry started to write it in 1519 while he was reading Martin Luther's attack on indulgences.

The king said that Luther...

> contemns the ancient Doctors of the church, and derides the new ones in the highest degree; loads with reproaches the Chief Bishop of the church. Finally, he so undervalues customs, doctrine, manners, laws, decrees and faith of the church (yea, the whole church itself) that he almost denies there is any such thing as a church, except perhaps such a one as himself makes up of two or three heretics, of whom himself is chief.[1]

Henry's book, dedicated to the pope, had two themes, both of which would turn out to be ironic—

the sanctity of marriage and the supremacy of the pope. Ironic, because Henry didn't honor the sanctity of his own marriage. He wanted to divorce his first wife, Catherine of Aragon, supposedly because she failed to produce a male heir to the throne. When the pope refused to annul the marriage, the king renounced the papacy's authority, and he consequently divorced her and married Anne Boleyn. In 1530, Henry was stripped of the title "Defender of the Faith" by Pope Paul III, after the king broke away from the Roman Catholic Church and established himself as the head of the new Church of England.

Thirteen years later, parliament gave the title back to the king. "Defender of the Faith" could not have been more inappropriate. Henry was not a man of faith, let alone a defender of it. Henry was known as a "lustful, egotistical, paranoid and tyrannical monarch," as well as an adulterer, who murdered his political opponents and beheaded two of his six wives. When Anne Boleyn also failed to give him a male heir, just as with Catherine, he accused her of adultery and had her executed.

His wives were not the only ones who met this fate. The History Channel called Henry "the most prolific serial killer England has known," having executed up to 57,000 people during his thirty-six year reign. Whether his once-loved wives, clergy, noblemen, or ordinary citizens, none were safe from his rage. The king perceived any who were against him to also be against God.[2]

Henry was the first to be given the royal title, which was then passed on to his successors. "Defender of the Faith" still speaks to the king's position as Supreme Governor of the Church of England.

In most of the fifteen Commonwealth countries, the phrase "Defender of the Faith" isn't used. Instead, the British king is given the title "By the grace of God." For example, in Australia Charles is proclaimed "King Charles the Third, by the Grace of God, King of Australia and his other Realms and Territories, Head of the Commonwealth." He is referred to as "Defender of the Faith" only in Canada, New Zealand, and the UK.

DEFENDER OF FAITH

In an official statement, the palace released a piece entitled "Will The Prince of Wales be 'Defender of Faith' or 'Defender of The Faith'?" In a 2015 interview, when the interviewer noted that Charles had previously described himself as merely "a defender of faith," Charles affirmed he would in fact be "Defender of the Faith":

No, I didn't describe myself as a defender: I said I would rather be seen as "Defender of Faith", all those years ago, because, as I tried to describe, I mind about the inclusion of other people's faiths and their freedom to worship in this country. And it's always seemed to me that, while at the same time being Defender of The Faith, you can also be protector of faiths. It was very interesting that 20 years or more after I mentioned this—which has been frequently misinterpreted—the Queen, in her Jubilee address to the faith leaders, said that as far as the role of the Church of England is concerned, it is not to defend Anglicanism to the exclusion of other religions. Instead, the Church has a duty to protect the free practice of all faiths in this country. I think in that sense she was confirming what I was really trying to say—perhaps not very well—all those years ago. And so I think you have to see it as both. You have to come from your own Christian standpoint—in the case I have as Defender of the Faith—and ensuring that other people's faiths can also be practiced.[3]

The Bible has much to say about kings and queens. Two of its major books are even titled "Kings." Some of the biblical monarchs had great faith, while others were completely godless. King David was a man of faith. King Saul was known for his interest in the occult and his rebellion against

God. King Ahab was known for his childish tantrums, while King Solomon is remembered for his wisdom, and for having a serious weakness for women—who brought about his downfall by leading him into the subtlety of idolatry.

We will now look at Queen Elizabeth II and consider her role as the Defender of the Faith, what that means, and what the role of King Charles will continue to be in the age of diversity and tolerance.

THE FAITH OF THE QUEEN

Queen Elizabeth II had an unashamed Christian faith that was evidenced throughout her life, both in her words and in her actions. Aside from her role as "Defender of the Faith and Supreme Governor of the Church of England," which came with the monarchy, her own personal faith was evident back in the early 1950s even before she was crowned queen. She said,

> Pray for me ... that God may give me wisdom
> and strength to carry out the solemn promises
> I shall be making, and that I may faithfully
> serve Him and you, all the days of my life.[4]

Her father, King George VI, had tragically passed away on February 6, 1952, while Elizabeth and her husband were in Kenya. She returned immediately, and was then crowned as Queen eighteen months later on June 2, 1953, at Westminster Abbey, London.

It is heartwarming to know that her Christmas broadcasts to her subjects were among the few speeches that she wrote herself. These frequently referred to Jesus, the founder of the Christian faith, whose birth is celebrated by millions at Christmas. During these special speeches, she often referred to her personal faith in Jesus. In her broadcast in December 2000, she stated, "For me the teachings of Christ and my own personal accountability before God provide a framework in which I try to lead my life."[5]

Her 1953 coronation was nothing like the contemporary world had ever seen. It was quite a spectacle with a glittering gold coach, kings, queens, princes and princesses, celebrities, and presidents from all around the world. There was an ancient throne, a royal sceptre, and a golden crown encrusted with 2,868 diamonds, 17 sapphires, 11 emeralds, and 269 pearls. All this, with an array of magnificent horses, marching soldiers in colorful uniforms, and the sounds of soul-stirring trumpet blasts. This was particularly meaningful because it came on the heels of the Second World War, which had left much of the country in ruins.

Here is the oath that Queen Elizabeth made before God as she began her seventy-year reign (taken from the Order of Service for the Coronation):

> The Archbishop standing before her shall administer the Coronation Oath, first asking the Queen,

Madam, is your Majesty willing to take the Oath?

And the Queen answering,

I am willing.

The Archbishop shall minister these questions; and The Queen, having a book in her hands, shall answer each question severally as follows:

Archbishop. Will you solemnly promise and swear to govern the Peoples of the United Kingdom of Great Britain and Northern Ireland, Canada, Australia, New Zealand, the Union of South Africa, Pakistan, and Ceylon, and of your Possessions and the other Territories to any of them belonging or pertaining, according to their respective laws and customs?

Queen. I solemnly promise so to do.

Archbishop. Will you to your power cause Law and Justice, in Mercy, to be executed in all your judgements?

Queen. I will.

Archbishop. Will you to the utmost of your power maintain the Laws of God and the true profession of the Gospel? Will you to the utmost of your power maintain in the United Kingdom the Protestant Reformed Religion established by law? Will you maintain and preserve inviolably the settlement of the Church of England, and the doctrine, worship, discipline, and government thereof, as by law established in England? And will you preserve unto the Bishops and Clergy of England, and to the Churches there committed to their charge, all such rights and privileges, as by law do or shall appertain to them or any of them?

Queen. All this I promise to do.

Then the Queen arising out of her Chair, supported as before, the Sword of State being carried before her, shall go to the Altar, and make her solemn Oath in the sight of all the people to observe the premises: laying her right hand upon the Holy Gospel in the great Bible (which was before carried in the procession and is now brought from the Altar by the Archbishop, and tendered to her as she kneels upon the steps), and saying these words:

The things which I have here before promised, I will perform and keep. So help me God.[6]

During her coronation, the orb, the scepter, the ring, and the crown used in the ceremony each include a cross to symbolize the supreme rule of Jesus Christ over the world. Even though the jewels in the crown are of great value, a Bible is presented to the queen during the coronation and described as "the most valuable thing that this world affords."

In a number of her Christmas speeches, she has referred to the story Jesus told of a "Good Samaritan," found in the Gospel of Luke. In 1985 she said that it "reminds us of our duty to our neighbour. We should try to follow Christ's clear instruction at the end of that story: 'Go and do thou likewise.'"[7]

In 1989 she said,

Many of you will have heard the story of the Good Samaritan, and of how Christ answered the question (from a clever lawyer who was trying to catch him out) "who is my neighbour?"...

It's not very difficult to apply that story to our own times and to work out that our neighbours are those of our friends, or complete strangers, who need a helping hand...It would be splendid to think that in the last years of the twentieth century Christ's message about loving our neighbors as ourselves might at last be heeded...In the hope that we will be kind and loving to one another, not just on

Christmas Day, but throughout the year, I wish you all a very Happy Christmas. God bless you.[8]

As well as unashamedly talking about her faith in Christ and regularly attending official church services, the Queen went to church privately each Sunday and said that she relied on the prayers of her people. In 1992, in a speech in which she marked the fortieth anniversary since her accession, she thanked those who had kept her in prayer, saying that it was those prayers that "sustained me through all these years."

Even in her more recent 2020 Christmas Eve message she continued to extol the principle of loving our neighbors as ourselves, stating:

> We continue to be inspired by the kindness of strangers and draw comfort that—even on the darkest nights—there is hope in the new dawn. Jesus touched on this with the parable of the Good Samaritan. The man who is robbed and left at the roadside is saved by someone who did not share his religion or culture. This wonderful story of kindness is still as relevant today. Good Samaritans have emerged across society showing care and respect for all, regardless of gender, race or background, reminding us that each one of us is special and equal in the eyes of God.[9]

Queen Elizabeth spoke not only of Jesus' teachings but also of His character. In 2008, she said:

> I hope that, like me, you will be comforted by the example of Jesus of Nazareth who, often in circumstances of great adversity, managed to live an outgoing, unselfish and sacrificial life...He makes it clear that genuine human happiness and satisfaction lie more in giving than receiving; more in serving than in being served.[10]

In 2012 the queen ended her Christmas message by suggesting a servant-hearted response to Jesus Christ's message of love:

> This is the time of year when we remember that God sent his only son "to serve, not to be served". He restored love and service to the centre of our lives in the person of Jesus Christ. It is my prayer this Christmas Day that his example and teaching will continue to bring people together to give the best of themselves in the service of others.
>
> The carol, "In the Bleak Midwinter", ends by asking a question of all of us who know the Christmas story, of how God gave himself to us in humble service: "What can I give him, poor as I am? If I were a shepherd, I would bring a lamb; if I were a wise man, I would do my part". The carol gives the answer, "Yet what I can I give him—give my heart".[11]

In 2011 the queen noted that "forgiveness lies at the heart of the Christian faith. It can heal broken families, it can restore friendships and it can reconcile divided communities. It is in forgiveness that we feel the power of God's love."[12]

In 2021 when her personal life was shaken by an interview given by Prince Harry and his wife, Meghan, her reaction was one of love and forgiveness. She said, "Harry, Meghan and Archie will always be much-loved family members."

The *Washington Post* said of the queen,

> At her coronation in 1953, Queen Elizabeth II was anointed with sacred oils by the archbishop of Canterbury and pledged to rule not just according to British laws, but the "laws of God," in her role as "Supreme Governor of the Church of England" and "Defender of the Faith."
>
> She was true to that vow. Her devotion to "Jesus Christ, Prince of Peace" was a fundamental and defining, though sometimes overlooked, pillar of her life.
>
> Now, as her son Charles III takes over, he has by all accounts accepted the responsibilities of his religious titles without reservation. But he will bring a markedly different personal vision of religion and spirituality to the role.[13]

CHAPTER TWO

THE QUEEN'S TREASURE HOUSE

To understand the role of the king to be the
Defender of the Faith, we need to look specifically at what it is that he is called to defend. He is to
contend for the faith, particularly for certain truths
given to us in the Bible. With those thoughts in
mind, we will look closely at the veneration given to
the Scriptures during Queen Elizabeth's coronation
in 1953. This is from the order of service for her coronation in Westminster Abbey:

> The Presenting of the Holy Bible
> When the Queen is again seated, the Arch-
> bishop shall go to her Chair; and the Moder-
> ator of the General Assembly of the Church of
> Scotland, receiving the Bible from the Dean of
> Westminster, shall bring it to the Queen and
> present it to her, the Archbishop saying these
> words:

Our gracious Queen:
to keep your Majesty ever mindful of the law
and the Gospel of God as the Rule for the
whole life and government of Christian
Princes, we present you with this Book,
the most valuable thing that this world
affords.

And the Moderator shall continue:
Here is Wisdom;
This is the royal Law;
These are the lively Oracles of God.[14]

Notice the honor given to the Bible. The archbishop told the queen to be ever mindful of its contents—the law and the gospel—as the rule for the whole life and the rule of governments, and of the fact that it is "the royal Law."

Queen Elizabeth once said, "To what greater inspiration and counsel can we turn than to the imperishable truth to be found in this treasure house, the Bible?"[15]

During her coronation it was called "the most valuable thing that this world affords." Therefore, when she laid her right hand upon the "Holy Gospel in the great Bible" it wasn't done lightly, because she saw it as a "treasure house." Three thousand years earlier, King David said a similar thing: "I rejoice at Your word as one who finds great treasure" (Psalm 119:162).

The queen was not alone in her esteem of the Scriptures. Patrick Henry stated, "Here is a Book worth more than all the other books which were ever printed." Abraham Lincoln said, "I believe the Bible is the best gift God has given to man...But for this Book, we could not know right from wrong... Take all you can of this Book upon reason, and the balance on faith, and you will live and die a happier man." Theodore Roosevelt noted that "a thorough understanding of the Bible is worth more than a college education," which Daniel Webster reiterated by saying that "education is useless without the Bible." Sir Isaac Newton said, "I have a fundamental belief in the Bible as the Word of God, written by men who were inspired. I study the Bible daily."

THE FORBIDDEN BOOK

The first Bible portion produced in the English language was translated from Latin and handwritten in 1382 by John Wycliffe, an Oxford professor, scholar, and theologian. He was well-known in Europe for opposing the teachings of the Catholic Church, which he saw as being contrary to the Scriptures. He produced dozens of English-language copies so the common people could read the Scriptures. Forty-four years after Wycliffe's death, the pope was so infuriated that he ordered Wycliffe's bones to be dug up, crushed, and thrown into the river.

According to *History Today*, Wycliffe had what the Catholic Church considered "startlingly unorthodox opinions," which the pope had condemned in 1377:

> Wycliffe...had come to regard the scriptures as the only reliable guide to the truth about God and maintained that all Christians should rely on the Bible rather than the unreliable and frequently self-serving teachings of popes and clerics. He said that there was no scriptural justification for the papacy's existence and attacked the riches and power that popes and the Church as a whole had acquired. He disapproved of clerical celibacy, pilgrimages, the selling of indulgences and praying to saints.[16]

One of John Wycliffe's followers was a priest named Jan Huss. He too believed that that people should be allowed to read the Bible in their own language, and that they should resist anyone in the Roman Catholic Church who threatened execution for possessing a Bible. The Catholic Church formally condemned Huss as a heretic, and he was handed over to the secular authorities to be burned at the stake on July 6, 1415.

> On the way to the place of execution, he passed a churchyard and saw a bonfire of his books. He laughed and told the bystanders not to believe the lies circulated about him. Arriving at the place of execution, he was asked by the empire's marshal if he would finally retract his views. Huss replied, "God is my wit-

ness that the evidence against me is false. I have never thought nor preached except with the one intention of winning men, if possible, from their sins. Today I will gladly die."[17]

A CENTURY LATER

Around one hundred years later in 1517, Martin Luther saw the same truths in Scripture. He went on to translate and publish the Bible in the commonly-spoken language of the German people. This was a courageous thing to do, because the torturing and killing of Christians was nothing new for the Catholic Church.

When William Tyndale translated and published the first-ever mechanically-printed New Testament in the English language in 1526, he paid dearly for that. At age forty-two he was tied to a stake, strangled, then his body burned for translating the Scriptures and daring to question the pope's authority.

The Vatican admits to the killing of Christians:

For centuries people were burned at the stake, stretched to death or otherwise tortured for failing to be Roman Catholic. But, if research released by the Vatican is right, the Inquisition was not as bad as one might think. According to the documents from Vatican archives relating to the trials of Jews, Muslims, Cathars, witches, scientists and other non-Catholics in Europe between the 13th and the 19th centuries, the number actually killed or tortured into confession during the Inquisition was far fewer than previously thought.

Estimates of the number killed by the Spanish Inquisition, which Sixtus IV authorized in a papal bull in 1478, have ranged from 30,000 to 300,000. Some historians are convinced that millions died.[18]

Suspected Protestants being tortured as heretics during the Spanish Inquisition.

Popes continued to forbid the reading of the Bible. Pope Pius IV compiled an *Index of Prohibited Books* and officially prohibited them at the Council of Trent in 1563. This is an excerpt:

> Whoever reads or has such a translation in his possession . . . cannot be absolved from his sins until he has turned in these Bibles . . . Books in the vernacular dealing with the controversies

between Catholics and the heretics of our time are not to be generally permitted, but are to be handled in the same way as Bible translations...[19]

However, the invention of the printing press by Johann Gutenberg was a gamechanger. Since the Bible first rolled off the press in the 1450s, today there are more than six billion Bibles in print in over 1,300 languages. The Harry Potter book series, by contrast, has sold 500 million.

The invention of the movable-type printing press meant that Bibles could be printed in large quantities in a short period of time. So now we can read "the most valuable thing that this world affords" without fear of being burned at the stake. And that brings us back to King Charles III and his role as Defender of the Faith.

CHAPTER THREE

ETERNAL LIFE, GOING CHEAP

It is important to remember that the title "Defender of the Faith" was originally given to Henry VIII as a reward for his defense of the Catholic Church. But when Henry parted with the Catholic Church, he was given the title as a defender of the Protestant Church, and the Protestant Church was to defend against what were seen to be the errors of Catholicism—particularly something called "indulgences." These were specifically objected to by Martin Luther. Of the practice, *Encyclopedia Brittanica* says,

> Those eager to gain plenary indulgences, but unable to go on pilgrimage to Jerusalem, wondered whether they might perform an alternative good work or make an equivalent offering to a charitable enterprise—for example, the building of a leprosarium or a cathedral. Churchmen allowed such commutation, and the popes even encouraged it, especially

Innocent III (reigned 1198–1216) in his various Crusading projects. From the 12th century onward the process of salvation was therefore increasingly bound up with money. Reformers of the 14th and 15th centuries frequently complained about the "sale" of indulgences by pardoners.[20]

In other words, if you had the means, you could buy eternal life by giving money to the Catholic Church. The *Washington Post* said,

Luther's objections to the Catholic Church's teachings on justification (how people are saved) came to a head over indulgences. At the time, indulgences could be purchased to grant remission of penalties for sins. Indulgences became a means of widespread economic exploitation, preying on the poor's fear of punishment in the afterlife.[21]

It is hard to believe, but indulgences are still part of the Catholic Church today:

The Church, then, teaches she has received from Christ, on the basis of the treasury of his merits, the power to grant to the faithful on certain conditions indulgences i.e. the remission of temporal punishment due to sin. Indulgences may be applied to the dead.[22]

The Encyclopedia Britannica also gives us background on Martin Luther:

By the end of 1518, according to most scholars, Luther had reached a new understanding of the pivotal Christian notion of salvation, or reconciliation with God. Over the centuries, the church had conceived the means of salvation in a variety of ways, but common to all of them was the idea that salvation is jointly effected by humans and by God—by humans through marshalling their will to do good works and thereby to please God and by God through his offer of forgiving grace. Luther broke dramatically with this tradition by asserting that humans can contribute nothing to their salvation: salvation is, fully and completely, a work of divine grace.

In essence, Luther realized the Bible said that eternal life came from God as a free gift—not something we earn based on religious works—while the Catholic Church taught that it was earned. What he said so infuriated the Church that they accused him of heresy and wanted to burn him at the stake. His intention was to reform the Catholic Church, but they would have no part of it, and so he took his 95 points of contention and famously nailed them to the door of a church in Wittenberg, Germany. That was the beginning of the Protestant Church.

National Geographic explained,

The Protestant Reformation began in Wittenberg, Germany, on October 31, 1517, when Martin Luther, a teacher and a monk, published a document he called *Disputation on the Power of Indulgences*, or 95 Theses. The document was a series of 95 ideas about Christianity that he invited people to debate with him. These ideas were controversial because they directly contradicted the Catholic Church's teachings.

Luther's statements challenged the Catholic Church's role as intermediary between people and God, specifically when it came to the indulgence system, which in part allowed people to purchase a certificate of pardon for the punishment of their sins. Luther argued against the practice of buying or earning forgiveness, believing instead that salvation is a gift God gives to those who have faith.[23]

The implications of what Luther discovered were massive. Either eternal life was a gift as the Bible says, or it could be purchased by indulgences and other religious practices. Which one is true? The fog lifts when we understand that God is a Judge, and we are criminals who have violated His perfect Law (the Ten Commandments). If that is the case, then anything we offer to Him is not good works, but an attempt to bribe Him, the ultimate Judge. Any criminal who offers a bribe to a good judge instantly digs himself into a seriously deeper hole—and God will *never* succumb to bribery. Our forgiveness could never be purchased. It could come only by the mercy of the Judge—through God's amazing grace. This is the teaching of the Bible:

> For by grace you have been saved through faith, and that not of yourselves; it is the gift of God, not of works, lest anyone should boast. (Ephesians 2:8,9)

Luther said,

We do not become righteous by doing righteous deeds but, having been made righteous, we do righteous deeds.

Unless I am convicted by Scripture and plain reason—I do not accept the authority of popes and councils, for they have contradicted each other—my conscience is captive to the Word of God. I cannot and will not recant anything, for to go against conscience is neither right nor safe. Here I stand, I cannot do otherwise. God help me. Amen.

My dear pope, I will kiss your feet and acknowledge you as supreme bishop if you will worship my Christ and grant that through His death and resurrection, not through keeping your traditions, we have forgiveness of sins and life eternal.

This is why the issue is so vitally important. If we believe eternal life can be earned, then we must labor to earn it or we will miss out on Heaven and end up in Hell. If, however, it's a gift, all we need to do is receive it through childlike faith—trusting alone in Jesus as Savior to wash away our sins. Good works then become acceptable, because they are an expression of gratitude, rather than an attempt at bribery. Here are some more Scriptures that speak of eternal life being the free gift of God:

> For the wages of sin is death, but the gift of God is eternal life in Christ Jesus our Lord. (Romans 6:23)

> But the free gift is not like the offense. For if by the one man's offense many died, much more the grace of God and the gift by the grace of the one Man, Jesus Christ, abounded to many. (Romans 5:15)

Should we zealously defend this truth—is it a hill on which to die? It certainly is—*if we care about the fate of those who believe that God can be bribed on Judgment Day*. Listen to the apostle Paul passionately defending the belief that we are saved without works. The Galatian church had turned away from salvation by grace, and instead thought they could be saved by their works:

> I marvel that you are turning away so soon from Him who called you in the grace of Christ, to a different gospel, which is not another; but there are some who trouble you and want to pervert the gospel of Christ. But even if we, or an angel from heaven, preach any other gospel to you than what we have

preached to you, let him be accursed. *As we have said before, so now I say again, if anyone preaches any other gospel to you than what you have received, let him be accursed.* (Galatians 1:6–9, emphasis added)

This is the apostle of love, the one who penned the beautifully famous words about love:

Though I speak with the tongues of men and of angels, but have not love, I have become sounding brass or a clanging cymbal. And though I have the gift of prophecy, and understand all mysteries and all knowledge, and though I have all faith, so that I could remove mountains, but have not love, I am nothing. And though I bestow all my goods to feed the poor, and though I give my body to be burned, but have not love, it profits me nothing. (1 Corinthians 13:1–3)

Yet he pronounced the terrible curse of God on *anyone* who changed the gospel of grace into what it's not. And that's exactly what the Roman Catholic Church has done, deceiving multitudes and deliberately keeping them in ignorance about how to be saved. Scripture warns,

None of them can by any means redeem
[either himself or] his brother,
Nor give to God a ransom for him—
For the ransom of his soul is too costly,
And he should cease trying forever—

So that he should live on eternally,
That he should never see the pit (grave) and
undergo decay. (Psalm 49:7–9, AMP)

Not only is it not possible to purchase redemption, but (again) for us guilty sinners to even offer God anything is exceedingly offensive:

The sacrifice of the wicked is hateful and exceedingly offensive to the LORD… (Proverbs 15:8, AMP)

Look at what happened in Scripture when someone thought he could purchase the gift of God:

But Peter said to him, "Your money perish with you, because you thought that the gift of God could be purchased with money! You have neither part nor portion in this matter, for your heart is not right in the sight of God. Repent therefore of this your wickedness, and pray God if perhaps the thought of your heart may be forgiven you. For I see that you are poisoned by bitterness and bound by iniquity." (Acts 8:20–23)

His attempt was seen as "wickedness." In reality, any righteousness we may have is likened to filthy rags: "But we are all like an unclean thing, and all our righteousnesses are like filthy rags…" (Isaiah 64:6).

But, the Catholic Church is adamant that our righteous works *are* acceptable. In fact, there are *seven* things they claim that must be done to be saved:

> Essential to the Roman Catholic doctrine of salvation are the Seven Sacraments, which are baptism, confirmation, the Eucharist, penance, anointing of the sick, holy orders, and matrimony. Protestants believe that, on the basis of faith in Christ alone, believers are justified by God, as all their sins are paid for by Christ on the cross and His righteousness is imputed to them. Catholics, on the other hand, believe that Christ's righteousness is imparted to the believer by "grace through faith," but in itself is not sufficient to justify the believer. The believer must supplement the righteousness of Christ imparted to him with meritorious works.[24]

Again, when does the offerer rest from his labors—has he ever done enough to earn eternal salvation? The answer is that those who are deceived by that false doctrine never know, and that is frightening. And there's one reason they stay deceived. That's what we will look at in the next chapter.

CHAPTER FOUR

THE CLASH WITH TRADITION

It was no wonder that Martin Luther was threatened with being burned at the stake when he began encouraging the common people to read the Scriptures. This is because the Bible reveals the many unbiblical practices of the Catholic Church. And the reason this deception continues is because most Roman Catholics don't tremble at God's Word. Church tradition often triumphs over the authority of Scripture, so for those who embrace them it's not important to handle the Bible with the utmost integrity. But like Queen Elizabeth, as she placed her hand on the "Holy Gospel in the great Bible," we must tremble at the very thought of misrepresenting what Scripture says:

> Hear the word of the LORD, you who tremble
> [with awe-filled reverence] at His word...
> (Isaiah 66:5, AMP)

...which untaught and unstable people twist to their own destruction, as they do also the rest of the Scriptures. (2 Peter 3:16)

We must never twist Scripture so that it says something that wasn't intended. If we do so, we do it to our own destruction. Take for instance the Catholic tradition of praying for the dead. The *Catholic News Herald* gives the reasons for this common practice:

According to the Catholic Encyclopedia, the clearest Bible reference about prayers for the dead is from the Second Book of Maccabees. When soldiers were preparing the bodies of their slain comrades for burial they discovered they were wearing amulets taken from a pagan temple which violated the law of Deuteronomy so they prayed that God would forgive the sin these men had committed.

The New Testament echoes this notion in the second letter of Timothy when Paul prays for someone who died named Onesiphorus, saying: "May the Lord grant him to find mercy from the Lord on that day."

The Catechism of the Catholic Church also has something to say about prayers for the dead, stating: "All who die in God's grace and friendship, but still imperfectly purified, are indeed assured of their eternal salvation; but after death they undergo purification, so as to achieve the holiness necessary to enter the joy of heaven."[25]

It states that Catholics pray for the dead because it's in the Bible. Actually, it's not: The books of 1 and 2 Maccabees are contained only in the Catholic Bible and are not recognized as canon by Protestants and Jews.

And the second justification given for praying for the dead is the second letter of Timothy, when "Paul prays for someone who died named Onesiphorus." But Scripture doesn't even hint at Onesiphorus being dead:

> The Lord grant mercy to the household of Onesiphorus, for he often refreshed me, and was not ashamed of my chain; but when he arrived in Rome, he sought me out very zealously and found me. The Lord grant to him that he may find mercy from the Lord in that Day—and you know very well how many ways he ministered to me at Ephesus. (2 Timothy 1:16–18)

It has been well said that the Bible is like a fiddle. You can play any tune you want on it ... if you have no fear of God. Each of us should take note of the men from Berea:

> Then the brethren immediately sent Paul and Silas away by night to Berea. When they arrived, they went into the synagogue of the

Jews. These were more fair-minded than those
in Thessalonica, in that they received the word
with all readiness, *and searched the Scriptures
daily to find out whether these things were so.*
(Acts 17:10,11, emphasis added)

The men of Berea didn't say, "This is the famous
apostle Paul" and then take whatever he said as
being gospel truth. Instead, they searched the Scriptures daily to find out whether these things were so.
You and I must do the same. Don't take my word for
it. Search the Scriptures and see if I'm telling you
the truth. Listen to the Scriptures again making it
clear that we are saved by God's grace without works
of righteousness:

> ...not by works of righteousness which we
> have done, but according to His mercy He

saved us, through the washing of regeneration and renewing of the Holy Spirit, whom He poured out on us abundantly through Jesus Christ our Savior, that having been justified by His grace we should become heirs according to the hope of eternal life. (Titus 3:5–7)

Look at the effect of the religious traditions of the scribes and the Pharisees at the time of Christ:

> Then the scribes and Pharisees who were from Jerusalem came to Jesus, saying, "Why do Your disciples transgress the tradition of the elders? For they do not wash their hands when they eat bread."
>
> He answered and said to them, "Why do you also transgress the commandment of God because of your tradition? For God commanded, saying, 'Honor your father and your mother'; and, 'He who curses father or mother, let him be put to death.' But you say, 'Whoever says to his father or mother, "Whatever profit you might have received from me is a gift to God"—then he need not honor his father or mother.' Thus you have made the commandment of God of no effect by your tradition. Hypocrites! Well did Isaiah prophesy about you, saying:
>
> 'These people draw near to Me with their mouth,
> And honor Me with their lips,

> But their heart is far from Me.
> And in vain they worship Me,
> Teaching as doctrines the commandments of
> men.'" (Matthew 15:1–9)

Jesus said, "Thus you have made the command-ment of God of no effect by your tradition. Hypo-crites!" They nullified the Scriptures in preference to their unbiblical traditions, and for it Jesus de-nounced them as "hypocrites."

If you study the Gospels you will see that Jesus was hounded because He continually violated their religious traditions—by healing on the Sabbath or for failing to ritualistically wash His hands before eating. The early church also had strong contentions with those who insisted that certain religious works were necessary to be saved:

> Some men came down from Judea and began
> teaching the brothers, "Unless you are circum-
> cised in accordance with the custom of Moses,
> you cannot be saved." Paul and Barnabas dis-
> agreed greatly and debated with them... (Acts
> 15:1,2, AMP)

Notice that Paul and Barnabas "disagreed greatly and debated with them." This was a *big* dispute. They were defending the faith. Salvation by grace alone was, and still is, a hill upon which to die. This is what they told them:

Now therefore, why do you test God by putting a yoke on the neck of the disciples which neither our fathers nor we were able to bear? *But we believe that through the grace of the Lord Jesus Christ we shall be saved...* (Acts 15:10,11, emphasis added)

THE DEATH OF STEPHEN

Stephen had been arrested for preaching the gospel. When he was asked to defend the faith, he concluded by saying,

> "You stiff-necked and uncircumcised in heart and ears! You always resist the Holy Spirit; as your fathers did, so do you. Which of the prophets did your fathers not persecute? And they killed those who foretold the coming of the Just One, of whom you now have become the betrayers and murderers, who have received the law by the direction of angels and have not kept it." (Acts 7:51–53)

God gave the Law to Moses, and instead of obeying it, the religious teachers ignored it and chose their own traditions over the Word of God. For being a defender of the faith, Stephen was murdered (see Acts 7:54–59).

There will forever be a clash between those who embrace their religious traditions thinking they can earn God's favor, and those who trust alone in His mercy. That clash began with the murder of Abel.

Cain thought he could earn God's favor by the works
of his own hands, while Abel trusted in a blood sacrifice. And because Cain's sacrifice was rejected by
God, he angrily killed his brother:

> By faith Abel offered to God a more excellent
> sacrifice than Cain, through which he obtained
> witness that he was righteous... (Hebrews
> 11:4)

Abel had faith, Cain had works:

> ...not as Cain who was of the wicked one and
> murdered his brother. And why did he mur-
> der him? Because his works were evil and his
> brother's righteous. Do not marvel, my breth-
> ren, if the world hates you. (1 John 3:12,13)

Keep in mind Jesus warned that hatred would
come from the religious:

> "And a time is coming when whoever kills you
> will think that he is offering service to God.
> And they will do these things because they
> have not known the Father or Me. I have told
> you these things [now], so that when their
> time comes, you will remember that I told you
> about them." (John 16:2–4, AMP)

The fact that everlasting life is a gift from God is
the ultimate good news. It's not something we have
to strive to earn, and this is good news for the whole
world, including Catholics, Muslims, Hindus,
Buddhists, and even for atheists. No one needs to lie

on beds of nails, sit on hard pews, crawl up steps of cathedrals until their knees bleed, or pay indulgences to religious hierarchy. All the suffering for our sin has already been done on the cross. The debt to the moral Law has been paid:

> For Christ also suffered once for sins, the just for the unjust, that He might bring us to God. (1 Peter 3:18)

When Jesus said, "It is finished" just before He died on the cross (see John 19:30), He was saying our sin debt is "Paid in full." Consider His words:

> "Come to Me, all you who labor and are heavy laden, and I will give you rest. Take My yoke upon you and learn from Me, for I am gentle and lowly in heart, and you will find rest for your souls. For My yoke is easy and My burden is light." (Matthew 11:28–30)

Jesus will give us rest from our labors. We don't need to labor to enter into Heaven, because entrance is free. All we have to do is yoke ourselves to Christ. Trust in Him for our eternity. This is the "rest" of which the Scriptures speak:

> For indeed we have had the good news [of salvation] preached to us, just as the Israelites also [when the good news of the promised land came to them]; but the message they heard did not benefit them, because it was not united with faith [in God] by those who heard.

For we who believe [that is, we who personal-
ly trust and confidently rely on God] enter
that rest [so we have His inner peace now
because we are confident in our salvation...].
(Hebrews 4:2,3, AMP)

If we think we are good enough to enter
Heaven, we will not trust in Christ alone, and that
will be to our damnation. That's why it's so important for King Charles to steadfastly remain as the
Defender of *the* Faith.

CHAPTER FIVE

CHARLES THE LIONHEART

It was understandable why Charles quipped that, as king, he would like to be the "defender of faith." We should all defend the right for everyone to believe as they will. But his *primary* duty is to defend the Protestant church against the errors of Catholicism—of the erroneous belief that salvation can be earned:

> The present position is that a British king cannot be a Roman Catholic, must be "in communion with" the Church of England, and swear that he is a faithful Protestant. Following the 1707 Act of Union between Scotland and England, he must, after accession, swear to "inviolably maintain and preserve" the Presbyterian form of church government established in the more autonomous Church of Scotland. This was one of Charles III's first acts as king.

The King's coronation consists of a service of Holy Communion, and a rite during which he is anointed and crowned by the Archbishop of Canterbury, primate of the Church of England. In coronation oaths prescribed by parliament in 1689, the King will swear, among other things, to "maintain and preserve inviolately" the establishment of the Church of England and the rights and privileges of its clergy.[26]

If the king isn't aware of the biblical aspects of these issues, it's understandable that he wouldn't want to be seen as a bigot. A *bigot*, according to the dictionary, is "a person who is obstinately or unreasonably attached to a belief, opinion, or faction, especially one who is prejudiced against or antagonistic toward a person or people on the basis of their membership of a particular group."

This issue isn't about "Protestantism." It's about preserving the integrity of the gospel—that eternal life is the gift of God. In that respect, *every* Christian should be an unashamed defender of the faith, even if the world hates us. Without a clear understanding that the issue of salvation is by grace through faith alone, it is easy to see how "Defender of *the* Faith" can be an uncomfortable title.

In speaking of Queen Elizabeth in that role, English editor, historian, commentator and writer Catherine Pepinster stated,

While it may surprise people, given the Queen's coronation oaths included upholding the Protestant religion, the signs are that the Queen has long been open to other faiths…

Mindful of Protestant sensitivities, she has been careful to visit Catholic churches in this country on rare occasions. On one occasion, she attended vespers in Westminster Cathedral but has never attended Mass in this country. Catholic Communion was, for hundreds of years, anathema to the Protestants of Britain who heard transubstantiation denounced as idolatrous, first in the coronation service and later in the accession statement, before mention of it finally disappeared.[27]

Think again of the indignation of the apostle Paul as he evoked the curse of God—damnation in Hell—against those who preach "another gospel." Adding to grace is adding poison to the cup of salvation. If anything should stir up wrath in the heart of King Charles, it should be the poison of salvation by works. He is sworn to be a defender of the biblical faith. Not a defender of other religious faiths, or even of social issues. They may be worthy causes, *but they have no bearing on the eternal salvation of sinners*. This does. Therefore, he should, with a ferocious indignation, guard the cup, and defend salvation by grace alone.

THE COAT OF ARMS

The royal coat of arms of the British monarch depicts nine lions, two of which are crowned and depict the authority of the king. It contains the motto *Dieu et mon droit* ("God is my right"). This symbol of divine authority has descended through the centuries to the present family:

> The Royal Arms were also used to symbolize the King's authority and, after Henry VIII became Supreme Head of the Church of England in 1534, they began to appear in churches, representing the connection between the monarch and the church.[28]

At first glance the two crowned lions on the royal arms are saying that the United Kingdom is a strong and conquering kingdom. But the message is deeper. It is that the king must be as bold as a lion. He must defend his territory.

A lion may look impressive but harmless—with his large mane and house cat–like features. Most of his day is spent lying under trees, yawning and sleeping. But in an instant, this kitty can become a terrifying and ferocious beast that will defend his territory to the death. No one in his right mind should step into the territory of a lion.

The role of the King of England is often one of pomp and ceremony. Despite his impressive crown, colorful robes, orb, swords, and scepter, we all know that he is just a figurehead. The king spends most of his day cutting ribbons and making warm speeches. But underneath all this, as Defender of the Faith, he is ferociously territorial. He has marked his territory, and any ugly hyenas who try to creep into his territory need to hear him roar, see his terrible teeth, and back off with their poisonous doctrine:

The king's wrath is like the roaring of a lion . . . (Proverbs 19:12)

Look at how King Solomon surrounded his throne with lions:

Moreover the king made a great throne of ivory, and overlaid it with pure gold. The throne had six steps, and the top of the throne was round at the back; there were armrests on either side of the place of the seat, and two lions stood beside the armrests. Twelve lions stood there, one on each side of the six steps; nothing like this had been made for any other kingdom. (1 Kings 10:18–20)

Salvation by grace alone *must* be defended with the utmost ferocity, and the crowned lions on the royal coat of arms are reminders for the king to be the Defender of the Faith.

THE LION OF JUDAH

Jesus was called the *Lion* of the tribe of Judah (Revelation 5:5) to display His absolute authority and the ferociousness of His wrath against sin:

> . . . when the Lord Jesus is revealed from heaven with His mighty angels, in flaming fire taking vengeance on those who do not know God, and on those who do not obey the gospel of our Lord Jesus Christ. These shall be punished with everlasting destruction from the presence of the Lord and from the glory of His power, when He comes, in that Day, to be glorified in His saints and to be admired among all those who believe, because our testimony among you was believed. (2 Thessalonians 1:8–10)

The Bible warns that it's a fearful thing to fall into the hands of the living God (Hebrews 10:31).

The apostle Paul said, "Knowing, therefore, the terror of the Lord, we persuade men" (2 Corinthians 5:11). The day will come when sinners will cry out in terror to the mountains and rocks, saying, "Fall on us and hide us from the face of Him who sits on the throne and from the wrath of the Lamb! For the great day of His wrath has come, and who is able to stand?" (Revelation 6:16,17).

Not only is Jesus called the King of kings, but He is called the Lord of lords, the one to whom every knee will bow:

> And He Himself will rule them with a rod of iron. He Himself treads the winepress of the fierceness and wrath of Almighty God. And He has on His robe and on His thigh a name written: KING OF KINGS AND LORD OF LORDS. (Revelation 19:15,16)

King Richard the Lionheart (1157–1199), an ancestor of Charles, was likened to a lion because of his courage and military might. May King Charles also be lionhearted, by fighting for the truths of the everlasting gospel.

Not many understand the hidden symbolism behind the British coronation. In the next chapter, we will reverently draw back the curtain and look at these fascinating symbols.

CHAPTER SIX

HIDDEN CORONATION SYMBOLISM

The crowning of a king is so uniquely magnificent, it's something the secular media can't ignore. In a world that has become secularized, the coronation serves as a powerful and sobering reminder of the existence of God:

> The coronation is an occasion for pageantry and celebration, but it is also a solemn religious ceremony. During the ceremony, the Sovereign takes the coronation oath—the form and wording have varied over the centuries.
>
> Today, the Sovereign undertakes to rule according to law, to exercise justice with mercy—promises symbolised by the four swords in the coronation regalia (the Crown Jewels)—and to maintain the Church of England. The Sovereign is then "anointed, blessed and consecrated" by the Archbishop,

whilst the Sovereign is seated in King Edward's chair (made in 1300, and used by every Sovereign since 1626). After receiving the orb and sceptres, the Archbishop places St Edward's Crown on the Sovereign's head. After homage is paid by the Archbishop of Canterbury and senior peers, Holy Communion is celebrated.[29]

In other words, in viewing the elaborate coronation ceremony, *the world is going to church*. And while watching, they will participate in a solemn service mentioning Jesus, the cross, the gospel, the Bible, the Ten Commandments (the Law), and the rule of God. The entire ceremony is filled with hidden symbolism that is based on the Bible. That's what we are going to look at in this chapter—ten weird facts about the coronation.

1. THE ROYAL ORB

While reporting on the funeral of Queen Elizabeth II, *CBS News* could not help but make reference to the Sovereign's orb. They had no choice, because this strange-looking ball was sitting precariously in front of her crown, beside her scepter, right on the top of the coffin. It was an elephant in the room. They therefore remarked:

The orb, also known as the Sovereign's Orb, is presented to the monarch during their coronation. This is called the investiture. The orb, which dates back to 1661, is a golden globe with a cross. It is meant to remind the monarch that their power is derived from God.[30]

The orb was originally made for Charles II's coronation in 1661. It is an 11.81 inch-wide (30 centimeter) hollow gold sphere, mounted with 9 emeralds, 9 sapphires, 18 rubies, 365 diamonds, 375 pearls, an amethyst, and a glass stone.

> The Sovereign's Orb, as this part of the Crown Jewels is officially named, is a symbol of Godly power. A cross above a globe, it represents "Christ's dominion over the world", as the Monarch is God's representative on Earth...
>
> It is presented to the Sovereign after they put on the Imperial Robe. The orb is brought from the altar by the Dean of Westminster, and given to the Archbishop of Canterbury to place into the Monarch's right hand. There he says: "Receive this orb set under the cross, and remember that the whole world is subject to the Power and Empire of Christ our Redeemer."[31]

The whole sinful world is indeed "subject to the power and empire of Christ our Redeemer":

The *globus cruciger* (Latin for "cross-bearing orb"), also known as "the orb and cross", is an orb surmounted by a cross... The cross represents Christ's dominion over the orb of the world, literally held in the hand of an earthly ruler.[32]

In the Bible, the book of Daniel prophesied of Christ's absolute dominion over all nations and of His everlasting Kingdom:

> "I saw in the night visions, and behold, with the clouds of heaven there came one like a son of man, and he came to the Ancient of Days and was presented before him. And to him was given dominion and glory and a kingdom, that all peoples, nations, and languages

should serve him; his dominion is an everlasting dominion, which shall not pass away, and his kingdom one that shall not be destroyed." (Daniel 7:13,14, ESV)

The apostle Paul also referenced this eternal kingdom—one which cannot be shaken: "Therefore, since we are receiving a kingdom which cannot be shaken, let us have grace, by which we may serve God acceptably with reverence and godly fear. For our God is a consuming fire" (Hebrews 12:28,29).

Those who trust in Jesus await the coming Kingdom in which He alone will reign supreme as King and Lord of all the earth. The orb is to remind the earthly king of that sobering fact.

2. THE SOVEREIGN'S SCEPTRE

The Sovereign's sceptre is a rod of authority held in the hand. It is a little weird for a king to be holding onto what is a stick of wood. This sceptre is reminiscent of the rod that Moses held in his hand: "But lift up your rod, and stretch out your hand over the sea and divide it. And the children of Israel shall go on dry ground through the midst of the sea" (Exodus 14:16).

Like the orb, the sceptre is also under the cross. It is one of two rods used in the coronation ceremony, representing the temporal power of the king or queen, and is associated with righteousness in governing.

As it is handed over to the Monarch, the Archbishop says: "Receive the rod of Equity and Mercy. Be so merciful that you be not too remiss; so execute justice that you forget not mercy. Punish the wicked, protect and cherish the just, and lead your people in the way wherein they should go."[33]

Equity is the impartial distribution of justice. And although it is referred to as a rod of equity, the king must always remember to show mercy. This is because the God of Justice remembered His great mercy toward humanity by providing a Savior:

> He has remembered His mercy and His faithfulness to the house of Israel; all the ends of the earth have seen the salvation of our God. (Psalm 98:3,4)

Equity demands that the scales of Justice be made equal. On the Day of Judgment, it will make sure that all evil is perfectly punished. The Scriptures continually warn us of coming equity for all of humanity: "For He is coming to judge the earth. With righteousness He shall judge the world, and the peoples with equity" (Psalm 98:9).

Scripture tells us that equity and justice are the very foundation of God's throne, and that "loyal love and faithfulness characterize [His] rule" (Psalm 89:14). Even though there have been many earthly kings, there is only one Sovereign, and He is the King of kings:

...our Lord Jesus Christ, which he will display at the proper time—he who is the blessed and only Sovereign, the King of kings and Lord of lords. (1 Timothy 6:15, ESV)

The fact that the sceptre indicates mercy within justice is exemplified in the biblical example of Queen Esther, who could approach the king's throne only when he held out his royal scepter toward her (see Esther 8:4).

Again, the scepter is also used to symbolize God's rule:

Your throne, O God, is forever and ever; a scepter of righteousness is the scepter of Your kingdom. (Psalm 45:6)

It is to remind the king of the mercy offered to us in the gospel, as well as of the second coming. That is when Jesus will return to earth and take His rightful place over the kingdoms of this world, and when "He will rule them with an iron scepter" (Revelation 19:15, NIV).

3. THE BLUNT SWORD OF MERCY

It is certainly strange that *three* swords are carried in front of the king as he enters Westminster Abbey: the blunt Sword of Mercy (also known as Curtana), the Sword of Spiritual Justice, and the Sword of Temporal Justice.[34] In addition to being the Defender of the Faith, the monarch also serves as the head of the British Armed Forces, and the swords reflect these roles.

When Adam and Eve sinned against God and brought death to the human race, God drove them out of the Garden of Eden and "[permanently] stationed the cherubim and the sword with the flashing blade which turned round and round [in every direction] to protect and guard the way (entrance, access) to the tree of life" (Genesis 3:24, AMP).

Through the cross, Jesus both satisfied the sharp Sword of Spiritual Justice and offers us the blunt Sword of Mercy: "Mercy and truth have met together; righteousness and peace have kissed" (Psalm 85:10).

4. THE SWORD OF SPIRITUAL JUSTICE

The Bible says that "the natural man does not receive the things of the Spirit of God, for they are foolishness to him; nor can he know them, because they are spiritually discerned" (1 Corinthians 2:14). For someone who was not "born of the Spirit," even the phrase "spiritual justice" sounds odd. However, justice is spiritual; it can't be seen. When the Bible speaks of God being "the habitation of justice" (Jeremiah 50:7), it is referring to God's invisible nature. We can see justice manifest in man's retribution for crime. But justice itself is spiritual, and the sharp and terrible swift sword of spiritual justice will be brought out on the Day of Judgment:

Mine eyes have seen the glory of the coming
of the Lord;
He is trampling out the vintage where the
grapes of wrath are stored;
He hath loosed the fateful lightning of His
terrible swift sword:
His truth is marching on.

5. THE SWORD OF TEMPORAL JUSTICE

Charles as the king must swear to uphold the civil
laws of the United Kingdom.

It is interesting to note that each of these three
swords is carried unsheathed and pointing upwards
during the coronation procession. It is perhaps
symbolic that all justice finds its roots in the Law
of God, and that the
wrath-filled divine
Law is unsheathed and
ready for action. God
has made ready His
sword:

If a man does not
repent, God will
sharpen His sword;
He has strung and
bent His [mighty]
bow and made it
ready. (Psalm 7:12,
AMP)

THE CORONATION TRUMPETS

It certainly is strange but soul-stirring to announce an event with a trumpet. We just don't do that in modern society. To blast a wedding gathering with trumpets as the bride enters the building would be overkill. It must be an event of events to justify the sound of a trumpet.

Many end-time events are heralded by a trumpet. One is the Day of the Lord (Joel 2:1; Zechariah 9:14–16), when Jesus Christ returns as King of kings and overthrows the nations of this world, establishing the Kingdom of God on earth. The resurrection from the dead is also connected to a mighty trumpet blast (1 Corinthians 15:52; 1 Thessalonians 4:16). While the book of Revelation tells of seven trumpets (Revelation 8:2–21; 11:15), when the last one sounds, "the kingdoms of this world have become the kingdoms of our Lord and of His Christ,

and He shall reign forever and ever!" (Revelation 11:15), indicating He has returned.

When King David gave instructions regarding the coronation of his son Solomon, he mentioned the trumpet: "There have Zadok the priest and Nathan the prophet anoint him king over Israel. Blow the trumpet and shout, 'Long live King Solomon!'" (1 Kings 1:34, NIV).

When Charles was proclaimed king following the death of his mother, there was a public fanfare of eight trumpets blaring from the palace balcony. In accordance with tradition, Charles was not present for the first part of the ceremony. The clerk of the council announced that "Prince Charles Philip Arthur George is now, by the death of our lady sov ereign of happy memory, become our King Charles III . . . God save the king!" Charles then joined them in the palace's crimson-and-gilt throne room, where he took the royal oath.

This is symbolic of another King, who though not physically present, will make His presence known with the sound of a trumpet:

Then the sign of the Son of Man will appear in heaven, and then all the tribes of the earth will mourn, and they will see the Son of Man coming on the clouds of heaven with power and great glory. And He will send His angels with a great sound of a trumpet, and they will gather together His elect from the four winds, from one end of heaven to the other. (Matthew 24:30,31)

7. THE CORONATION CHAIR

The coronation chair is certainly a curiosity. One would think that a king or queen would be crowned on a magnificent throne. Instead, they are crowned on what is basically a plain, old wooden chair. Kept in Westminster Abbey, this ancient chair is where British monarchs sit when they are crowned at their coronations. To date, twenty-six monarchs, including Queen Elizabeth II, have been crowned on this chair since it was commissioned in 1296 by King Edward I. Underneath the seat of the chair

is a large stone known as the "Stone of Scone."

8. THE CORONATION ANOINTING

When planning the 1953 coronation of Queen Elizabeth, there was talk of allowing television cameras into Westminster Abbey. Winston Churchill was horrified at the thought. He told the House of Commons, "It would be unfitting that the whole ceremony, not only in its secular but also in its religious and spiritual aspects, should be presented as if it were a theatrical performance."[35]

But it was broadcast. All of it... except for one very sacred moment. And this, of all the rituals and symbolism, is strange, particularly to those who have never read the Bible:

> The Act of Consecration is the most magical aspect of an English Coronation, so extraordinary that history (and the 1953 Coronation Committee) decreed it must remain out of sight.
>
> In preparation, the Queen was disrobed of her crimson cloak, her jewellery was removed and the young Elizabeth was seated in King Edward's chair, an ancient and simple throne, clothed in a dress of purest white. It was a moment of high theatre.
>
> A golden canopy held by four Knights of the Garter was suspended above and around the monarch, a grander version of the cloth cabinet a conjuror might wheel onto stage before making his glamorous assistant disappear.
>
> With the Abbey almost silent, the Archbishop of Canterbury was handed the Ampulla, a flask in the shape of an eagle wrought in solid gold.[36]

This most sacred part of the coronation ceremony takes place before the investiture and crowning.

> From the flask, the archbishop poured some "blessed oil" of orange, roses, cinnamon, musk and ambergris, and anointed the Queen in the form of a cross, on the palms of her hand, on the breast and on the crown of her head.
>
> As he did so, he whispered these words: "Be thy head anointed with holy oil: as kings, priests, and prophets were anointed. And as Solomon was anointed king by Zadok the priest and Nathan the prophet, so be you anointed, blessed and consecrated Queen over the Peoples, whom the Lord thy God hath given thee to rule and govern."[37]

The anointing of the sovereign is based on the anointing of kings in the Old Testament. Anointing began with Israel's first king, Saul (see 1 Samuel 10:1–27). David was also anointed with oil: "Then Samuel took the horn of oil and anointed him in the midst of his brothers; and the Spirit of the LORD came upon David from that day forward" (1 Samuel 16:13).

This anointing indicates that the individual is God's chosen vessel, and the person must be submitted to God who chose them for that role.

9. THE KING'S SIX CORONATION ROBES

One odd but integral part of the splendor is the apparel worn by those involved in the coronation—especially that of the king. Few people realize that there are six robes worn by the sovereign during the ceremony.

When Charles enters Westminster Abbey, he will be wearing the Robe of State (or Parliament Robe). During the investiture he will don the Colobium Sindonis with the Supertunica worn over it. On top of that will be the Robe Royal, worn as he is crowned. At the conclusion of the coronation the king will be wearing the Imperial Robe, also known as the Robe of Estate, indicating his priestly role and the divine nature of kingship.[38]

> The order in which the robes are worn was established for Edward II's 1308 coronation in the 14th century manuscript *Liber Regalis* (Latin for "Royal Book")...
>
> During the part of the ceremony known as the anointing, the monarch is divested of all celebrated symbols of status, and wears the *Colobium Sindonis* (Latin for "Shroud Tunic"). In stark contrast to the Robe of State, this gown is austere and plain, without detail or lace. In its simplicity, this robe symbolizes divesting oneself of all worldly vanity, to stand bare before God.[39]

In Genesis 2:25, we are told that Adam and Eve were naked and unashamed. However, after they sinned against God, their eyes were opened and they were ashamed (see Genesis 3:7). When the Bible speaks of "nakedness" before God, it is speaking of the shame of our sins:

"...that you may be clothed, that the shame of your nakedness may not be revealed." (Revelation 3:18)

Jesus spoke of a man who tried to enter Heaven without a covering:

"But when the king came in to see the guests, he saw a man there who did not have on a wedding garment. So he said to him, 'Friend, how did you come in here without a wedding garment?' And he was speechless. Then the king said to the servants, 'Bind him hand and foot, take him away, and cast him into outer darkness; there will be weeping and gnashing of teeth.'" (Matthew 22:11–13)

Just as the father put a robe over the prodigal son to cover his filth (see Luke 15:22), when we come to Christ, we are robed in His righteousness, so that our sin and shame aren't seen by God. We are washed clean of our filthiness solely by the grace of God—without any works on our part:

Do you not know that the unrighteous will not inherit the kingdom of God? Do not be

deceived. Neither fornicators, nor idolaters…
will inherit the kingdom of God. And such
were some of you. But you were washed, but
you were sanctified, but you were justified in
the name of the Lord Jesus and by the Spirit
of our God. (1 Corinthians 6:9–11)

10. THE ROYAL CROWN

St Edward's Crown is the centerpiece of the Crown
Jewels of the United Kingdom. It is named after
Edward the Confessor (1003–1066), and variations
of it have traditionally been used at coronations
since the thirteenth century.

St Edward's Crown, used to crown English
monarchs, was considered to be a holy relic,
kept in the saint's shrine at Westminster
Abbey and therefore not worn by monarchs at
any other time. Instead, a "great crown" with
crosses and fleurs-de-lis, but without arches
(an open crown), was a king's usual headgear
at state occasions until the time of Henry V,
who is depicted wearing an imperial crown of
state with gold arches (a closed crown). Arches
were a symbol of sovereignty, and by this
point in history, the king of England was
being celebrated as *rex in regno suo est impera-
tor*—an emperor of his own domain—owing
obedience to no one but God.[40]

It is odd that instead of one cross, as we often
see on Christian church buildings, there are *four*

crosses on the nearly five-pound (2.23 kg) St Edwards' crown. These are perhaps symbolic of the four Gospels of Matthew, Mark, Luke, and John. Or they may speak of the universal nature of the gospel, where the faithful come from the four corners of the earth:

> They will come from the east and the west, from the north and the south, and sit down in the kingdom of God. (Luke 13:29)

And of course, the four crosses on the crown remind us of another crown. It is the painful crown of thorns Jesus wore in the cross. After Adam sinned, God cursed the ground of the earth with thorns and thistles (see Genesis 3:17,18). Jesus' suffering on the cross would redeem us from the curse of the Law:

> Christ has redeemed us from the curse of the law, having become a curse for us... (Galatians 3:13)

The brilliant Isaac Watts (1674–1748) called the crown of thorns a "rich" crown:

> See from His head, His hands, His feet,
> Sorrow and love flow mingled down!

Did e'er such love and sorrow meet,
Or thorns compose so rich a crown?[41]

And now believers eagerly watch the signs of the times and wait, praying for the coming kingdom:

"Your kingdom come. Your will be done on earth as it is in heaven." (Matthew 6:10)

Remember Jesus said to enter that Kingdom we must be born again: "Most assuredly, I say to you, unless one is born again, he cannot see the kingdom of God... Do not marvel that I said to you, 'You must be born again'" (John 3:3,7).

We will be born again when we forsake our own efforts (good works), repent of our sins, and trust alone in Jesus for our salvation. Then, as the apostle Paul so aptly said, we groan as we await that day:

For we know that the whole creation groans and labors with birth pangs together until now. Not only that, but we also who have the firstfruits of the Spirit, even we ourselves groan within ourselves, eagerly waiting for the adoption, the redemption of our body. (Romans 8:22,23)

It is then that the Kingdom will come and God's will, will be done on earth as it is in Heaven. At that time, "God will wipe away every tear from their eyes; there shall be no more death, nor sorrow, nor crying. There shall be no more pain, for the former things have passed away" (Revelation 21:4).

As we watch the magnificent splendor of the coronation of an earthly king, we must never forget that all this pageantry is nothing but a very, very faint shadow of the glory that is to come:

> ...the twenty-four elders fall down before Him who sits on the throne and worship Him who lives forever and ever, and cast their crowns before the throne, saying:
>
> "You are worthy, O Lord,
> To receive glory and honor and power;
> For You created all things,
> And by Your will they exist and were created." (Revelation 4:10,11)
>
> "...and of His kingdom there will be no end." (Luke 1:33)

CHAPTER SEVEN

THE CONFESSION OF A PRINCE

A sk around about whether character is important when it comes to our political leaders, and you'll get a varied response. Should presidents and kings be held to a higher moral standard than the average person on the street? Is character in leadership important? Of course it is. We want those we look to as leaders to be honest and faithful. However, it's easy to lose sight of that ideal and to become disillusioned and even cynical by how many leaders have fallen into adultery.

One of those who fell was King Charles, and it happened when he was a prince. This wasn't a nebulous rumor in a sordid tabloid headline. It was made public across the globe by Charles himself, and it's hard to erase the image of him confessing on international television that he had been unfaithful to his wife.

The Prince of Wales has admitted publicly for the first time that he was unfaithful to the Princess of Wales, ITN claimed last night.

But he was unfaithful only after his marriage had disintegrated beyond repair, possibly as late as 1992, according to News at Ten. It said he had made his infidelity clear in the documentary about his life to be shown on Wednesday.

The makers of Wednesday's program by Central Television, entitled "Charles: the Private Man, the Public Role," have done their utmost to keep the contents secret after being granted unprecedented access to the Prince over more than a year. It has been portrayed by royal observers as part of a Palace "charm offensive" to rebuild the Prince's image after his damaging separation from the Princess in 1992, 11 years after they married. It is also seen as the latest installment in the public relations campaign being fought between the estranged couple.[42]

But Charles wasn't the only guilty party in the marriage:

Far from the perfect marriage that most people expected from the Royal couple, Prince Charles and Princess Diana faced many problems in their marriage. The couple both admitted to being unfaithful to one another.[43]

It is true that time helps most of us to forgive, but we're not as quick to forget:

It took years for many in Britain to forgive Charles for his admitted infidelity to Diana before "the people's princess" died in a Paris car crash in 1997. But the public mood softened after he married Camilla Parker Bowles in 2005 and she became the Duchess of Cornwall.

Although Camilla played a significant role in the breakup of Charles and Diana, her self-deprecating style and salt-of-the-earth sense of humor eventually won over many Britons.

She helped Charles smile more in public by tempering his reserve and made him appear approachable, if not happier, as he cut ribbons, visited houses of worship, unveiled plaques and waited for the crown.

Her service was rewarded in February 2022, when Queen Elizabeth II said publicly that it was her "sincere wish" that Camilla should be known as "Queen Consort" after her son succeeded her, answering questions once and for all about her status in the Royal Family.[44]

One can't help but remember the famous biblical story of the woman who was caught in the act of adultery, and how the stone-throwers were ready with stones in hand. It was early in the morning when Jesus sat down and taught in the temple:

> Then the scribes and Pharisees brought to Him a woman caught in adultery. And when they had set her in the midst, they said to Him, "Teacher, this woman was caught in adultery, in the very act. Now Moses, in the law, commanded us that such should be stoned. But what do You say?" This they said, testing Him, that they might have something of which to accuse Him. But Jesus stooped down and wrote on the ground with His finger, as though He did not hear.
>
> So when they continued asking Him, He raised Himself up and said to them, "He who is without sin among you, let him throw a stone at her first." And again He stooped down and wrote on the ground. Then those who heard it, being convicted by their conscience, went out one by one, beginning with the oldest even to the last. And Jesus was left alone, and the woman standing in the midst. When Jesus had raised Himself up and saw no one but the woman, He said to her, "Woman, where are those accusers of yours? Has no one condemned you?"
>
> She said, "No one, Lord."

And Jesus said to her, "Neither do I condemn you; go and sin no more." (John 8:3–11)

Such a moving story of love and forgiveness
should leave us thinking about our own sins, especially in the light of these powerfully convicting
words Jesus spoke in the Sermon on the Mount:

> "You have heard that it was said to those of
> old, 'You shall not commit adultery.' But I say
> to you that whoever looks at a woman to lust
> for her has already committed adultery with
> her in his heart." (Matthew 5:27,28)

I remember as a twenty-two-year-old surfer
reading those words back in 1972. I was a young
businessman who was clean-cut and friendly. But
no one saw that my heart was filled with unlawful
sexual desire. Like every other red-blooded male, I
lived for the pleasure of lust. As the Scriptures appli-
cably describe our prowling as "having eyes full
of adultery and that cannot cease from sin, enticing
unstable souls" (2 Peter 2:14).

No one knew the pleasures that continually
filled my sinful heart. Not my friends, family, or my
beloved bride of two years. As I read the Bible that
night, the words that Jesus spoke about adultery
gave me comfort, because I had never committed
adultery. My thought was that if Heaven existed, I
would get there because I had been faithful to my
wife—although I had felt the power of temptation. I
owned a combined surf-shop and leatherwear store.

For two years I had been making dressy leather jackets to order for customers, and every now and then a woman would ask me to make her a miniskirt. I would find myself measuring the waist of a woman I didn't know, and then measuring the length down to her thigh, and hearing a whisper, telling me how easy it would be to commit adultery. No one would know if I slapped a "Back Soon" note on the door of my store. That never happened, but I remember feeling the darkness of my own sinful heart.

That's why I thought that I would make it to Heaven, because I had resisted the temptation. But then I read what Jesus said next: "But I say to you that whoever looks at a woman to lust for her has already committed adultery with her in his heart." Those words cut into my very soul. It was as though an arrow plunged into my heart. I thought, "Oh no!! God sees my thought-life. He knows exactly what has gone on in my mind. I am condemned. I'm undone. I won't make it to Heaven! What should I do?" That's when I first understood the cross. Oh the relief, and the gratitude to God for His kindness in not treating me according to my sins, and instead granting me everlasting life as a free gift.

Therefore, because my many sins had been forgiven, I must be forgiving of Charles. I dare not point a holier-than-thou finger. None of us can. None of us can throw stones at others, because none of us are without sin. And it seems I'm not alone in my forgiving attitude:

Approval ratings for King Charles have soared "through the roof" since his accession to the throne. The boost in public favor is said to have come as a product of the King's public interaction throughout the 10-day mourning period and his open displays of grief in wake of Queen Elizabeth II's death. In the days following the Queen's death, 63 percent of those polled by YouGov believed King Charles III would make a good monarch, up from just 32 percent who believed the same in May of this year.[45]

KING DAVID AND ADULTERY

There was another king who, many years ago, fell sexually. He had hit the media headlines as a hero in Israel—for famously taking down a giant of a man named Goliath. King David had been walking on the rooftop of his castle, when he saw a neighbor's attractive wife bathing herself. Rather than look away, he coveted his neighbor's wife—in direct violation of the Tenth Commandment:

> You shall not covet your neighbor's house; you shall not covet your neighbor's wife, nor his male servant, nor his female servant, nor his ox, nor his donkey, nor anything that is your neighbor's. (Exodus 20:17)

And as the Bible says, lust brings forth sin (see James 1:15). He took her to himself *knowing* that she was married to another man, and he had sex with her. Unfortunately, she became pregnant with the king's child. And so David had a dilemma. How could he cover his sin? If it was leaked, there would be a royal scandal. Instead of killing the innocent child (as happens so often nowadays through abortion), David had her innocent husband killed. It seemed to have worked. The scandal had been averted. But there was a bigger scandal looming that David apparently didn't take into account: God had seen his sin, and He wasn't happy.

We pick up the story when God sent Nathan, a faithful prophet, to confront the king. Nathan began by telling David a story about a rich man and a poor man. The rich man had massive flocks, and the poor man had nothing except one beloved lamb, which he raised as a child. The pet even ate the man's food and drank from his own cup as it lay in his lap—it was like a daughter to him. Then Nathan said that a traveler came to the rich man, and instead of taking from his own flock to feed him, the rich man took the poor man's beloved lamb, killed it, and fed it to the stranger:

> So David's anger was greatly aroused against the man, and he said to Nathan, "As the LORD lives, the man who has done this shall surely die! And he shall restore fourfold for the lamb, because he did this thing and because he had no pity."

Then Nathan said to David, "You are the man! Thus says the LORD God of Israel: 'I anointed you king over Israel, and I delivered you from the hand of Saul. I gave you your master's house and your master's wives into your keeping, and gave you the house of Israel and Judah. And if that had been too little, I also would have given you much more! Why have you despised the commandment of the LORD, to do evil in His sight? You have killed Uriah the Hittite with the sword; you have taken his wife to be your wife, and have killed him with the sword of the people of Ammon. Now therefore, the sword shall never depart from your house, because you have despised Me, and have taken the wife of Uriah the Hittite to be your wife.' Thus says the LORD: 'Behold, I will raise up adversity against you from your own house; and I will take your wives before your eyes and give them to your neighbor, and he shall lie with your wives in the sight of this sun. For you did it secretly, but I will do this thing before all Israel, before the sun.'"

So David said to Nathan, "I have sinned against the LORD."

And Nathan said to David, "The LORD also has put away your sin; you shall not die. However, because by this deed you have given great occasion to the enemies of the LORD to blaspheme, the child also who is born to you shall surely die." (2 Samuel 12:5–14)

How quick David was to condemn that rich man for his sin, and how quick we all are to pick up stones. We have a tragic propensity to judge others harshly and not see our own sinful hearts.

Notice that God didn't strike down David—as He killed a man in the book of Genesis because He didn't like what he did sexually (see Genesis 38:6–10). Instead, He showed him mercy—after David acknowledged his sin. That's when Nathan said, "The LORD also has put away your sin; you shall not die." And look closely at the penitent prayer that then issued from the king's heart:

Have mercy upon me, O God,
According to Your lovingkindness;
According to the multitude of Your tender
mercies,
Blot out my transgressions.
Wash me thoroughly from my iniquity,
And cleanse me from my sin.
For I acknowledge my transgressions,
And my sin is always before me.
Against You, You only, have I sinned,
And done this evil in Your sight—
That You may be found just when You speak,
And blameless when You judge. (Psalm 51:1–4)

David *owned* his sin. He didn't call it a "weakness" or a "mistake." He called it what it was; it was "evil" in the sight of God.

Perhaps Charles prayed something similar when his sin was exposed. I certainly did the night my sin was exposed. Whatever the case, the Scriptures tell us that the shame Charles brought upon himself will always be remembered:

Whoever commits adultery with a
woman lacks understanding;
He who does so destroys his own soul.
Wounds and dishonor he will get,
And his reproach will not be wiped away.
(Proverbs 6:32,33)

King Charles may be forgiven by God, but it will always be a stain upon his reputation. It is a tragic wound and dishonor. I certainly hope that the sorrow he showed in his public confession was a sorrow that he had sinned against God, and that he had consequently found a place of repentance and faith in Jesus. However, sad as it is to say, there is a possibility that he may only have an intellectual faith in Christ, rather than a living relationship (as a result of the new birth of John chapter 3). While we cannot judge another human being, we can see what's in the heart by listening to what comes out of the mouth. In September 13, 2022, a faulty pen revealed what was in the heart of the then new king...

CHAPTER EIGHT

THE PEN THAT LEAKED THE KING'S HEART

Just after Charles became king, his patience and depth of godliness was tested when he used a pen that unfortunately let him down:

> Drats! King Charles III experienced a snafu with a leaky pen during a signing ceremony in Northern Ireland—and the monarch was less than pleased.
>
> "Oh G-d, I hate this thing!" Charles, 73, quipped as a pen leaked all over his hand while signing a visitor's book at Hillsborough Castle on Tuesday, September 13.
>
> The monarch quickly stood up and handed the pen to his wife as he rubbed his fingers clean. "Oh look, it's everywhere," Queen Consort Camilla, 75, said as she inspected the pen, to which the king replied, "I can't bear this

bloody thing...every stinking time," before exiting the room.

The sovereign was also frustrated due to initially signing the wrong date on the documents before checking with an aide who alerted him that he was a date behind.[46]

Most would say that using God's name in vain is just a mild form of cussing. Everybody does it. Nowadays, it's culturally acceptable. However, Scripture says differently: "For they speak against You wickedly; Your enemies take Your name in vain" (Psalm 139:20).

I was speaking to a young man who felt terrible that he had taken the Lord's name in vain, and he offered the excuse that when it's all around you, you just can't help but join in and speak in such a way. So I said, "If everybody around you used your *mother's* name as a cuss word, would you join in?" He was quick to say that he wouldn't—he could never do such a thing. To use God's name in vain, to use it lightly, to use it as a cuss word, or to fail to give it due honor is a violation of the Third Commandment:

> You shall not take the name of the LORD your God in vain, for the LORD will not hold him guiltless who takes His name in vain. (Exodus 20:7)

Often, those who use God's name in a blasphemous way don't even realize they are doing it. And that's the essence of what it means to "take it in vain." It is to count it as worthless, running off their lips without a second thought.

Perhaps Charles saw himself on television that evening, using the Lord's name in such a way, and sought God for forgiveness. We don't know. We would hope so. We want the King of England to be a godly man—a man of character who fears God— because "it is an abomination for kings to commit wickedness, for a throne is established by righteousness" (Proverbs 16:12).

Listen to what Jesus said about the fear of the Lord:

> "Therefore do not fear them. For there is nothing covered that will not be revealed, and hidden that will not be known.
>
> "Whatever I tell you in the dark, speak in the light; and what you hear in the ear, preach on the housetops. And do not fear those who kill the body but cannot kill the soul. But rather fear Him who is able to destroy both soul and body in hell." (Matthew 10:26–28)

It's a fearful thing to fall into the hands of God, and our hearts tremble for those who will find themselves in their sins on Judgment Day. And while we would far rather talk about the love of God, we cannot ignore His justice.

Immediately after Jesus spoke of the reality of Hell, He spoke of the love of God, using the common sparrow to illustrate God's love for you, me, and King Charles:

> "Are not two sparrows sold for a copper coin? And not one of them falls to the ground apart from your Father's will. But the very hairs of your head are all numbered. Do not fear therefore; you are of more value than many sparrows.
>
> "Therefore whoever confesses Me before men, him I will also confess before My Father who is in heaven. But whoever denies Me before men, him I will also deny before My Father who is in heaven." (Matthew 10:29–33)

That's my hope—that King Charles is not ashamed to confess his faith before men—that he truly is the Defender of the Faith. In recent years he courageously attempted to draw attention to an unfashionable cause, one that is often dismissed: the persecution of Christians around the world. It's difficult to pinpoint the moment he publicly became an advocate for the cause of suffering Christians around the world. However, he did make a public declaration in 2013 regarding ISIS persecuting Christians in Syria and Iraq. It was then that the prince visited a Coptic Orthodox Church center and a Syrian Orthodox Church in southern England. They hosted a reception for Middle East Christians in Clarence House, his London residence. During that time, his office released this statement:

"The Prince has expressed concern about the current challenges facing Christians in some Middle Eastern nations and wanted to meet members of those communities resident in the UK to find out more ," his office explained at the time. "The Prince of Wales wants to draw attention to the importance of harmony and understanding between peoples of all faiths."[47]

Prince Charles urged Christians in the United Kingdom not to take for granted their freedoms to practice their faith. He issued a clear warning, after meeting with Christian children who were forced to leave their homes following violent conflicts in Iraq and Syria. He said: "It is heart-breaking beyond words to see just how much pain and suffering is being endured by Christians in this day, simply because of their faith. As Christians we remember of course how our Lord called upon us to love our enemies and to pray for those who persecute, but for those confronted with such hatred and oppression I can only begin to imagine how incredibly hard it must be to follow Christ's example."[48]

He has said the following to faith leaders in September 2022:

> My Lord Archbishop, Dean, Ladies and Gentlemen. I am very grateful to have had this opportunity to meet you all, so soon after my Accession, in what are inevitably the saddest of circumstances for me and my Family. I have been touched by your kind words of condolence more than I can possibly say. They mean a great deal to me.
>
> I also wanted, before all of you today, to confirm my determination to carry out my responsibilities as Sovereign of all communities around this country and the Commonwealth and in a way which reflects the world in which we now live.
>
> I am a committed Anglican Christian, and at my Coronation I will take an oath relating to the settlement of the Church of England. At my Accession, I have already solemnly given—as has every Sovereign over the last 300 years—an Oath which pledges to maintain and preserve the Protestant faith in Scotland.

I have always thought of Britain as a "community of communities." That has led me to understand that the Sovereign has an additional duty—less formally recognized but to be no less diligently discharged. It is the duty to protect the diversity of our country, including by protecting the space for Faith itself and its practise through the religions, cultures, traditions and beliefs to which our hearts and minds direct us as individuals. This diversity is not just enshrined in the laws of our country, it is enjoined by my own faith. As a member of the Church of England, my Christian beliefs have love at their very heart. By my most profound convictions, therefore—as well as by my position as Sovereign —I hold myself bound to respect those who follow other spiritual paths, as well as those who seek to live their lives in accordance with secular ideals.

The beliefs that flourish in, and contribute to, our richly diverse society differ. They, and our society, can only thrive through a clear collective commitment to those vital principles of freedom of conscience, generosity of spirit and care for others which are, to me, the essence of our nationhood. I am determined, as King, to preserve and promote those principles across all communities, and for all beliefs, with all my heart.

This conviction was the foundation of everything my beloved mother did for our country, over her years as our Queen. It has been the foundation of my own work as Prince of Wales. It will continue to be the foundation of all my work as King.[49]

In the next chapter, we will look at an amazing lesson King Charles (and you and I) can learn from the wisest of all kings—King Solomon.

CHAPTER TEN

KING SOLOMON'S CORONATION

The Bible tells us that when Solomon became king, he was anointed with oil and the people shouted, "Long live King Solomon!" This was followed by great rejoicing:

> Then Zadok the priest took a horn of oil from the tabernacle and anointed Solomon. And they blew the horn, and all the people said, "Long live King Solomon!" And all the people went up after him; and the people played the flutes and rejoiced with great joy, so that the earth seemed to split with their sound. (1 Kings 1:39,40)

The phrase "Long live the king!" is used to express support for the heir who succeeds to the throne after the previous monarch has died.

Three thousand years later, the coronation of Charles has striking similarities. The *Independent* had an article titled "'Long live the King!' Trumpets and tears as thousands gather to see Charles III proclaimed monarch," describing the pomp and ceremony:

> Large crowds gathered outside St James's Palace on Saturday morning to sing and cheer as King Charles III formally ascended to the throne.
>
> They stood below the famed balcony in Friary Court to witness a man whose title is the garter king of arms come out and proclaim the new monarch following a formal ceremony inside.
>
> State trumpeters sounded the royal salute before the King's Guard gave three cheers—Bearskin hats raised with each one—and a rousing rendition of the national anthem was performed.
>
> And the thousands here loved every moment.[50]

We can learn a lot from Solomon. He was said to be the wisest man to ever live, but look at what happened:

> But King Solomon loved many foreign women, as well as the daughter of Pharaoh: women of the Moabites, Ammonites, Edomites, Sidonians, and Hittites—from the nations of whom the LORD had said to the children of Israel, "You shall not intermarry with them, nor they with you. Surely they will turn

Solomon receiving envoys of the tributary nations

away your hearts after their gods." Solomon
clung to these in love. And he had seven hundred wives, princesses, and three hundred
concubines; and his wives turned away his
heart. For it was so, when Solomon was old,
that his wives turned his heart after other
gods; and his heart was not loyal to the LORD
his God, as was the heart of his father David...

So the LORD became angry with Solomon, because his heart had turned from the
LORD God of Israel, who had appeared to him
twice, and had commanded him concerning
this thing, that he should not go after other
gods; but he did not keep what the LORD had
commanded. (1 Kings 11:1–4,9,10)

While the lesson for us is to be careful of sexual
sin, the life of King Solomon has an even greater les-

son. It is to be careful of the subtle sin of idolatry. Notice that Scripture once again speaks of salvation with reference to the Kingdom of God, and who will enter that coming Kingdom:

> Now the works of the flesh are evident, which are: adultery, fornication, uncleanness, lewdness, idolatry,...and the like; of which I tell you beforehand, just as I also told you in time past, that those who practice such things will not inherit the kingdom of God. (Galatians 5:19–21)

Following the list of sexual sins is the word "idolatry." Idolatry is when someone has his own image of God. And those who create a god to suit themselves will not only feel at liberty to give themselves to sexual sin, but they will more often than not create their own way to obtain salvation.

But to be a Defender of the Faith means to uphold the central doctrine of the exclusivity of Christ. This is arguably the most uncomfortable part of the commission of King Charles, as it is with almost every Christian. The exclusivity of Christ is the politically incorrect conviction that faith in Jesus is the *only* way to God. This is a biblical doctrine that may be offensive to the world, but Scripture gives no wiggle-room for the believer:

> "I am the way, the truth, and the life. No one comes to the Father except through Me." (John 14:6)

Nor is there salvation in any other, for there is no other name under heaven given among men by which we must be saved. (Acts 4:12)

Whoever transgresses and does not abide in the doctrine of Christ does not have God. (2 John 9)

The apostle Paul goes even further, saying that the things the Gentiles sacrifice "they sacrifice to demons and not to God, and I do not want you to have fellowship with demons" (1 Corinthians 10:20).

In today's climate of professed tolerance, it's not at all popular to say that Jesus is the only way to God. How dare we say that Christianity alone is right, and the billions of sincere Hindus, Buddhists, Muslims, and all the other religious followers are wrong. While each of us should have the right to believe what we will, *this* belief—that Jesus is the *only* way—understandably sends up the bristles. However, there is a way to be true to Scripture and at the same time help it make sense. It is to look to the message of the gospel. So I will take a few moments to present it to you in the hope that it not only makes sense, but that through it you will find assurance of eternal life. So let's make sure you're right with God—that you're "born again," as Jesus said you must be to enter the Kingdom of God (see John 3:3).

Do you think you are a good person? No doubt, like most of us, you do. How many lies do you think you have told in your life? Have you ever stolen something, even if it's small? If you've done these two things, then you are a lying thief. Have you ever used God's name in vain, either flippantly (including "OMG") or as profanity? If you have, let me ask you if you would ever use your mother's name as a cuss word. I'm sure you wouldn't, because that would show you don't respect her in the slightest. And yet you have used God's holy name as a cuss word. That's called "blasphemy," and it's very serious in God's eyes. He promises that whoever takes His name in vain will not be guiltless. One more question. Jesus said that if we look with lust we commit adultery in our heart. Have you ever looked at someone with lust? If you're normal, you have.

So here is a summation of your court case on Judgment Day. You have admitted to being a lying, thieving, blasphemous adulterer at heart. When God judges you by the Ten Commandments, are you going to be innocent or guilty? Guilty, of course. Will you therefore go to Heaven or Hell? The answer is that if you die in your sins, you have God's promise that you will end up in Hell. The Bible says that all liars will be cast into the lake of fire, and no thief, no adulterer, and no blasphemer will inherit the Kingdom of God.

Does that make you fearful? If it does, that's good. Fear is doing its beneficial work. It's being your friend, not your enemy, by showing you that you desperately need God's mercy. It's also humbling you so that you will be able to understand the good news of the gospel—that, although the wages of sin is death, God offers you the gift of everlasting life in Jesus Christ, the Savior.

Here is the good news: The Ten Commandments are God's "moral Law." You and I broke the Law, but Jesus paid the fine in His life's blood. That's what happened when He died on the cross. That's why He said just before He died, "It is finished!" In other words, the debt has been paid in full. If you're in court and someone pays your fine, the judge can let you go even though you are guilty. In doing so, he still does what is legal, right, and just. Does that make sense? Even though you are guilty, you are free to walk out of the courtroom, because someone has paid your fine. The Bible says, "God demonstrates His own love toward us, in that while we were still sinners, Christ died for us" (Romans 5:8). God proved His great love for you through the cross. Then Jesus rose from the dead, and defeated the power of the grave.

It is because Jesus paid the fine for sin on the cross that God can dismiss your case. You can walk out of His courtroom on Judgment Day. He can pardon your death sentence and legally let you live forever, all because Jesus paid the fine for sin in full on that cross. God has made the way to find everlasting life so simple that a child can understand it.

All you need to do is be honest and humble. You simply have to repent of your sins and trust in Jesus alone. Repentance means to turn from sin. You can't say you're a Christian and continue to lie, steal, and blaspheme God's holy name. That would be to deceive yourself and play the hypocrite. Your repentance must be sincere to be genuine. Then you trust in Jesus alone for your salvation, as you would trust in a parachute.

Today, repent and trust in Jesus, because the reality is, you may not have tomorrow. If you're not sure how to repent, here is a model prayer of repentance, given to us in Scripture when King David had his sin exposed:

> Have mercy upon me, O God, According to Your lovingkindness; according to the multitude of Your tender mercies, blot out my transgressions. Wash me thoroughly from my iniquity, and cleanse me from my sin. For I acknowledge my transgressions, and my sin is always before me. Against You, You only, have I sinned, and done this evil in Your sight—that You may be found just when You speak, and blameless when You judge. (Psalm 51:1–4)

We all have a multitude of sins, and for those who would try to deny that, the proof of the serious nature of our sin will be our death. It is *appointed* for men to die once and then face judgment (see Hebrews 9:27). Solomon warned, "For God will bring every work into judgment, including every secret thing, whether good or evil" (Ecclesiastes 12:14).

Every human being who has died *will* be raised from the dead:

> Do not marvel at this; for the hour is coming in which all who are in the graves will hear His voice and come forth—those who have done good, to the resurrection of life, and those who have done evil, to the resurrection of condemnation. (John 5:28,29)

On that great and terrible day, only those who are morally clean in God's sight will escape the wrath of His Law.

When Moses once asked to see God's glory, He told him that he couldn't see Him and live. However, He hid Moses in the cleft of a rock, and allowed him to look at where He had been. The reason Moses was hidden in a cleft of a rock was because God's goodness would kill him in an instant.

Imagine a judge has a heinous criminal in front of him who has raped, tortured, and then murdered a number of innocent little girls. If that judge is a good man, his goodness will be revealed in his anger toward the wicked criminal. In the same way, the goodness of God is revealed in His anger against evil. Sinners cannot stand in His holy presence without being immediately killed—*because of His goodness*. Look at the wording of Scripture in that passage:

> And he [Moses] said, "Please, show me Your glory."
>
> Then He said, "*I will make all My goodness pass before you*, and I will proclaim the name of the LORD before you. I will be gracious to whom I will be gracious, and I will have compassion on whom I will have compassion." But He said, "You cannot see My face; for no man shall see Me, and live." And the LORD said, "Here is a place by Me, and you shall stand on the rock. So it shall be, while My glory passes by, that I will put you in the cleft of the rock, and will cover you with My hand while I pass by. Then I will take away My hand, and you shall see My back; but My face shall not be seen." (Exodus 33:18–23, emphasis added)

That's the God we must face on Judgment Day, and unless we are hidden in Jesus (the Rock of Ages), God's goodness will fall on us like lightning and consume us in wrath:

> Rock of ages cleft for me
> Let me hide myself in Thee
> …Nothing in my hand I bring
> Simply to Thy cross I cling

We bring nothing in our hand. No religious works. Look at the Bible's description of that terrible day:

> Then I saw a great white throne and Him who sat on it, from whose face the earth and the heaven fled away. And there was found no place for them. And I saw the dead, small and great, standing before God, and books were opened. And another book was opened, which is the Book of Life. And the dead were judged according to their works, by the things which were written in the books. The sea gave up the dead who were in it, and Death and Hades delivered up the dead who were in them. And they were judged, each one according to his works. Then Death and Hades were cast into the lake of fire. This is the second death. And anyone not found written in the Book of Life was cast into the lake of fire. (Revelation 20:11–15)

How do we get our names written into the Book of Life? Is it by offering this holy God the abomination of what we think are good works? No. A thousand times no. We are saved by Jesus through the new birth. No one else can save us—only God's "Son from heaven, whom He raised from the dead, even Jesus who delivers us from the wrath to come" (1 Thessalonians 1:10).

All the major religions of the world are similar to Catholicism, in that they say we have to "do" something to be saved. We have to pray, to fast, to face a certain direction, do penance, give money, do good works, etc. But anything we offer God isn't a sacrifice, it's a bribe. It's an abomination to Him. He will not pervert justice on that Day. If we are guilty in court with no means of justification, the sensible thing to do is to throw ourselves on the mercy of the judge. And the Bible says that God is "rich in mercy" (Ephesians 2:4). The Judge disrobed, came down from the bench, and paid our fine so that we could leave the courtroom. He provided the payment— the perfect sacrifice of the sinless Lamb of God. We don't have to do anything, because God did everything for us. He gets the praise; we don't. He saves us, not because we are good, but because *He* is good and kind, and rich in mercy. This is incredibly good news for Catholics, Hindus, Muslims, Buddhists, atheists, agnostics, and for very other human being who desperately wants to find everlasting life. Death has lost its terrible sting...all because of the cross. This is what Peter preached two thousand years ago:

> "The sun shall be turned into darkness,
> And the moon into blood,
> Before the coming of the great and awesome
> day of the LORD.
>   And it shall come to pass
> That whoever calls on the name of the LORD
> Shall be saved." (Acts 2:20,21)

Whoever calls on the name of the Lord shall be saved. That's *not* exclusive, as some claim. "Whoever" is an open invitation to anyone...even you and me. Again, that means Catholics, Hindus, Muslims, Buddhists, atheists, agnostics, etc., can repent and trust in Jesus *alone* for the gift of salvation.

> And the Spirit and the bride say, "Come!" And let him who hears say, "Come!" And let him who thirsts come. Whoever desires, let him take the water of life freely. (Revelation 22:17)

May King Charles III never be deceived by idolatry and, like Solomon, go after other gods. May he never fail in his oath to be like Jesus, a true and faithful witness (see Revelation 1:5; 3:14).

May Charles be the Defender of the Faith. Long live the king.

"Honor the king." (1 Peter 2:17)

NOTES

1. Excerpt from William L. Sachse, Ed., "The Defense of the Seven Sacraments," *English History in the Making* Vol I (New York: John Wiley and Sons, 1967), 182–183 <luminarium.org/renlit/defense.htm>.
2. "The killer king: How many people did Henry VIII execute?" Sky HISTORY TV Channel <history.co.uk/article/the-killer-king-how-many-people-did-henry-viii-execute>.
3. "Will The Prince of Wales be 'Defender of Faith' or 'Defender of The Faith'?" <princeofwales.gov.uk/will-prince-wales-be-defender-faith-or-defender-faith>.
4. Christmas Broadcast 1952 <royal.uk/queens-first-christmas-broadcast-1952>.
5. Christmas Broadcast 2000 <royal.uk/christmas-broadcast-2000>.
6. The Queen's Coronation Oath, 1953 <royal.uk/coronation-oath-2-june-1953>.
7. Christmas Broadcast 1985 <royal.uk/christmas-broadcast-1985>.
8. Christmas Broadcast 1989 <royal.uk/christmas-broadcast-1989>.
9. The Christmas Broadcast 2020 <royal.uk/christmas-broadcast-2020>.
10. Christmas Broadcast 2008 <royal.uk/christmas-broadcast-2008>.
11. Christmas Broadcast 2012 <royal.uk/christmas-broadcast-2012>.
12. Christmas Broadcast 2011 <royal.uk/christmas-broadcast-2011>.
13. Kevin Sullivan and Michelle Boorstein, "King Charles III may bring new approach to 'Defender of the Faith,'" *Washington Post*, September 13, 2022.
14. "The Form and Order of Service that is to be performed and the Ceremonies that are to be observed in The Coronation of Her Majesty Queen Elizabeth II in the Abbey Church of St.

Peter, Westminster, on Tuesday, the second day of June, 1953" <oremus.org/liturgy/coronation/cor1953b.html>.

15. Dudley Delffs, "Died: Queen Elizabeth II, British Monarch Who Put Her Trust in God," September 8, 2022 <christianity today.com/news/2022/september/obit-queen-elizabeth-ii-personal-faith-christian-bible.html>.

16. Richard Cavendish, "John Wycliffe condemned as a heretic," *History Today*, Vol. 65 Iss. 5, May 2015 <historytoday.com/archive/john-wycliffe-condemned-heretic>.

17. Ken Curtis, Ph.D., "John Hus: Faithful unto Death," ChristianityToday.com, May 3, 2010 <christianity.com/church/church-history/timeline/1201-1500/john-hus-faithful-unto-death-11629878.html>.

18. Sophie Arie, "Historians say Inquisition wasn't that bad," *The Guardian*, June 15, 2004 <theguardian.com/world/2004/jun/16/artsandhumanities.internationaleducationnews>.

19. Hans J. Hillerbrand, *The Reformation* (London: SCM Press Ltd and Harper and Row, Inc., 1964).

20. Lawrence G. Duggan, "indulgence," *Encyclopedia Britannica* <britannica.com/topic/indulgence>.

21. Mika Edmondson, "How the Protestant Reformation led to Martin Luther King, Jr.," *The Washington Post*, January 14, 2017 <washingtonpost.com/news/acts-of-faith/wp/2017/10/31/how-the-protestant-reformation-led-to-martin-luther-king-jr>.

22. Indulgences," Catholic Online <catholic.org/prayers/indulg.php>.

23. The Protestant Reformation," *National Geographic* <education.nationalgeographic.org/resource/protestant-reformation>.

24. "What are the differences between Catholics and Protestants?" Got Questions? <gotquestions.org/difference-Catholic-Protestant.html>.

25. "Why do we pray for the dead?" *Catholic News Herald*, March 27, 2017; updated November 10, 2021 <catholicnewsherald.com/faith/funeral/204-news/grief-header/1577-why-do-we-pray-for-the-dead>.

26. Bob Morris, "King Charles, defender of faith: what the monarchy's long relationship with religion may look like under the new sovereign," The Conversation, September 20, 2022 <theconversation.com/amp/king-charles-defender-of-faith-

what-the-monarchys-long-relationship-with-religion-may-look-like-under-the-new-sovereign-190766>.

27. Catherine Pepinster, "Defender of the Faith: How the Queen's engagement with faith has shaped a twenty-first century Church of England," Theos, January 6, 2022 <theos-thinktank.co.uk/comment/2022/05/31/defender-of-the-faith-how-the-queens-engagement-with-faith-has-shaped-a-twentyfirst-century-church-of-england>.

28. Royal Coat of Arms," Britroyals <britroyals.com/arms.asp>.

29. The King's Body Guard of the Yeomen of the Guard <yeomenoftheguard.co.uk/coronations>.

30. Caitlin O'Kane, "As the U.K. mourns Queen Elizabeth II, here are some symbols in the events and what they represent," CBS News, September 12, 2022 <cbsnews.com/news/queen-elizabeth-ii-crowns-crown-jewels-orb-scepter-paddington-corgis-marmalade-sandwiches/>.

31. Victoria Howard, "Symbols of Monarchy: the orb and sceptre," The Crown Chronicles, August 20, 2016 <thecrownchronicles.co.uk/explanation/symbols-of-monarchy-sovereigns-orb-and-sceptre>.

32. "Globus Cruciger," Wikipedia <en.wikipedia.org/wiki/Globus_cruciger>.

33. Victoria Howard, "Symbols of Monarchy."

34. "Crown Jewels of the United Kingdom," Wikipedia <en.wikipedia.org/wiki/Crown_Jewels_of_the_United_Kingdom>.

35. Mark Easton, "Coronation 1953: Magic moment the TV cameras missed," BBC News, June 4, 2013 <bbc.com/news/uk-22764987>.

36. Ibid.

37. "The Coronation Spoon," Royal Collection Trust <rct.uk/collection/31733/the-coronation-spoon>.

38. Amanda Jones, "King Charles, His Six Coronation Robes, and their Symbolism," La Voce di New York, September 21, 2022 <lavocedinewyork.com/en/news/2022/09/21/king-charles-his-six-coronation-robes-and-their-symbolism>.

39. Ibid.

40. "Imperial State Crown," Wikipedia <en.wikipedia.org/wiki/Imperial_State_Crown>.

41. Isaac Watts, "When I Survey the Wondrous Cross," 1707 <en.wikipedia.org/wiki/When_I_Survey_the_Wondrous_Cross>.

42. Marianne Macdonald, "Prince of Wales admits adultery," The Independent, June 27, 1994 <independent.co.uk/news/prince-of-wales-admits-adultery-1425497.html>.

43. Busayo Ogunjimi, "Princess Diana Claimed Charles' Adultery Affected the Lives of Their Sons When It Was Disclosed," Feb. 06, 2022, AmoMama <news.amomama.com/286078-princess-diana-claimed-charles-adultery.html>.

44. "After Lifetime of Preparation, Charles Takes the British Throne | Chicago News," AP, September 8, 2022 <news.wttw.com/2022/09/08/after-lifetime-preparation-charles-takes-british-throne>.

45. Leia Paxton, "King Charles approval ratings 'through the roof' after dramatic surge in public support," Express, Sept. 21, 2022 <express.co.uk/news/royal/1672055/King-Charles-royal-family-public-approval-YouGov-Camilla-Queen-Consort-poll-vn>.

46. Kat Pettibone, "King Charles III Gets Frustrated Over a Faulty Pen During Signing Ceremony in Ireland: 'Oh G-d, I Hate This,'" US Magazine, September 13, 2022, <usmagazine.com/celebrity-news/news/king-charles-iii-frustrated-over-faulty-pen-at-ireland-ceremony>.

47. Luke Coppen, "King Charles III, defender of persecuted Christians," The Pillar, September 13, 2022 <pillarcatholic.com/king-charles-iii-defender-of-persecuted-christians>.

48. "Prince Charles: don't take your Christian freedoms for granted," Premier Christian News, December 19, 2017 <premierchristian.news/en/news/article/prince-charles-don-t-take-your-christian-freedoms-for-granted>.

49. Ibid.

50. Colin Drury, "'Long live the King!' Trumpets and tears as thousands gather To See Charles III Proclaimed Monarch," The Independent, September 10, 2022 <independent.co.uk/news/uk/home-news/charles-king-proclaimed-london-palace-b2164382.html>.